With Love,
from me ... to me

With Love, from me ... to me

A LETTER TO MY SIXTEEN-YEAR-OLD SELF

Edited by Joseph Galliano
Foreword by Miriam O'Callaghan

TRANSWORLD IRELAND

TRANSWORLD IRELAND
an imprint of The Random House Group Limited
20 Vauxhall Bridge Road, London SW1V 2SA
www.rbooks.co.uk

First published in 2010 by Transworld Ireland,
a division of Transworld Publishers

Selection © Joseph Galliano 2010
Foreword © Miriam O'Callaghan 2010
Letters © individual contributors 2010

Joseph Galliano has asserted his right under the Copyright, Designs
and Patents Act 1988 to be identified as the editor of this work.

A CIP catalogue record for this book
is available from the British Library.

ISBN 9781848271036

Every effort has been made to obtain the necessary permissions with reference to copyright
material, both illustrative and quoted. We apologize for any omissions in this respect and
will be pleased to make the appropriate acknowledgements in any future edition.
All images, excluding personal photos and letters, courtesy of Shutterstock.
Cartoon of Ross O'Carroll Kelly © Alan Clarke.
Sonia O'Sullivan photos © Evening Echo/Irish Examiner
Oscar Wilde photo © Napoleon Sarony / Bridgeman Art Library

Addresses for Random House Group Ltd companies outside the UK
can be found at: www.randomhouse.co.uk
The Random House Group Ltd Reg. No. 954009

The Random House Group Limited supports the Forest Stewardship
Council (FSC), the leading international forest-certification organization. All our
titles that are printed on Greenpeace-approved FSC-certified paper carry the FSC logo.
Our paper procurement policy can be found at
www.rbooks.co.uk/environment

Printed and bound in Great Britain by
Butler Tanner & Dennis Ltd, Frome

2 4 6 8 10 9 7 5 3 1

Contributors

Maeve Binchy

Charlie Bird

Mary Black

John Boyne

Jason Byrne

David Coleman

Richard Corrigan

Bill Cullen

Ray D'Arcy

Rosanna Davison

Damien Dempsey

Ian Dempsey

Christy Dignam

Tom Dunne

Dustin the Turkey

Julie Feeney

Ray Foley

Tony Griffin

Sean Hughes

Róisín Ingle

Jennifer Johnston

Gerald Kean

Brian Keenan

Cathy Kelly

Frank Kelly

John Kelly

Brian Kennedy

Mary Kennedy

Jon Kenny

Derek Landy

Jackie Lavin

Neven Maguire

Maser

Nell McCafferty

Colum McCann

Barry McGuigan

Paddy Moloney

Patrick Monahan

Kevin Myers

Anna Nolan

Rebecca Nolan

Paul Noonan

David Norris

Miriam O'Callaghan

Ross O'Carroll Kelly

Joseph O'Connor

Colm O'Gorman

Ardal O'Hanlon

Sonia O'Sullivan

Feargal Quinn

John Rocha

Adi Roche

Andrea Roche

Patricia Scanlan

Jason Sherlock

Victoria Smurfit

Sister Stan

Kathryn Thomas

John Waters

Foreword

Do you ever think back on your sixteen-year-old self? What you were like – what you might say to yourself if you met that person now?

Why not try something? Pick up a pen, take some paper, sit down and write a letter to that sixteen-year-old. Think about who you were as a teenager, and then put the words 'Dear Me' at the top of the page and just write.

That's the task that was set for some of Ireland's more well-known people and the results are gathered here – they are a surprisingly good read. At times they are funny, thoughtful, moving, uplifting, sad and unexpected. But why sixteen? It's a funny age, when children aspire to adulthood. Too many grown ups spend their time chasing their lost youth. Sixteen is the crossroads, a hinterland between those worlds where we are neither adult nor child. We are younger than we'd like to realize and yet adult responsibilities are already bearing down.

At sixteen, anything and everything is possible. Life can take so many turns. I was studying law at University College Dublin at sixteen – no clue there of how my life would end up. But I know I was lucky, because I was given the opportunity of a fine education from my hard-working parents – and that's a gift I am eternally grateful for.

It's the reason I got involved in this project. This book has a purpose: its primary aim is to raise funds for the Irish Youth Foundation, and the royalties are going to that foundation so that less fortunate young people are given the best opportunities in life. The Irish Youth Foundation funds many grassroots projects that enable hundreds of disadvantaged teenagers to fulfil their potential, including youth clubs, organizations that help young people keep away from crime and drugs, education classes and groups serving children with special needs.

Every sixteen-year-old deserves the same opportunities in life, every sixteen-year-old deserves to be loved and nurtured, and every sixteen-year-old deserves to be told and to believe that they can pursue their dreams and that no one or no thing will stand in their way.

I hope you enjoy this book. Miriam O'Callaghan

"To get back my youth I would
do anything in the world,
except take exercise, get up early,
or be respectable."

Oscar Wilde

JOHN BOYNE
www.johnboyne.com

Dublin, 10 July 2010

Dear John

Stop looking so bloody miserable all the time. You're not going to be any more popular, any better looking or any funnier by going round with a look on your face that would turn milk sour. If you don't have as many friends as you want, go out and make some more. If you feel lonely all the time, get out of the house once in a while. But enough with the moaning, yeah? It's depressing me.

Some answers to questions you're wondering about:
— You're right, you won't miss school when you leave. Actually, you'll never give it a second thought afterwards.
— No, there's nothing wrong with you just because you want to be Kylie's friend but you want to be Jason's friend even more. All of that's going to work out just fine in the end.
— Yes, you should join the drama society and not hover outside the door every day, too nervous to go in. You'll regret this one, John. But you've got another year to set it right. So join the drama society. Do it now. NOW. Be an actor. Or try to be one anyway.

And some advice:

- Don't buy any more albums by any of these people: Sonia, Rick Astley, Brother Beyond. Although feel free to continue insisting that life as a 16 year-old is depressing enough without having to listen to The Smiths all the time.
- Stop playing piano, start playing guitar.
- Take better care of all those short stories you're writing. I know that USB Drives haven't been invented yet but you might want to look back at them someday.
- Invent the USB Drive.

And one tip:

- Not to get all Marty McFly on you but 16 years from now, on January 20th 2003, you're going to be leaving work and a gang will be going for a drink. Make sure you go with them. Under no circumstances go home. Your entire future happiness will depend on this.

And one last thing, since it will take you 20 years to fully understand: it's only "it's" if it means "it is", otherwise it's always "its"

Big love!

John

Chernobyl Children's
Project International

"Offering Hope
To Live"

Dingle 23 July 2010

Dear Me

Hold your horses! Exams aren't everything! However, it wouldn't be any harm to focus your mind on Peig and not expect your mother to learn it for you! For starters you could switch off your tranny and put away the 'Spotlight' magazine! Other than that, you are doing absolutely fine as you are – you're a loyal friend and good person – believe in yourself. This is a wonderful time in your life – you're on the threshold of 'flying the nest'.

Now I'm not trying to put 'an old head on young shoulders' but could you 'lighten up' in relation to worrying about how you look and are you as good as everyone else – you are your own unique, quirky self! You are made of the right stuff and come from good strong stock – from a people who had a deep sense of moral responsibility, along with a keen sense of justice, instilled in you by your parents and grandparents. Your father's drive and belief that anything was possible if one applied oneself was a paramount philosophy of life that you have inherited – you're learning through your mum and dad that not everyone is equal and that will give you a deep sense of responsibility towards the rights of others. These are your most formative years and please relax, be happy in the knowledge that these qualities will be your greatest resource throughout your life.

Let me leave you with a beautiful Jewish proverb and call on it throughout your life: 'One heart is mirror to another'....remember that and be happy in the knowledge that it's a privilege to lend a helping hand, a real gift, you have lots to do young lady Adi so relax and enjoy the journey!

PEACE

Adi x xx

Adi

Adi

Roche

Bill Cullen
The Boss

Office Of The Apprentice
Europa Academy
Balheary Road
Swords, Co. Dublin
Ireland
Tel: +353.1.883 9200
Fax: +353.1.883 9247
Email: bill@glencullen.ie

From Bill "Liam" Cullen

Hi Liam

Just looking at the photo of you when you were sixteen with eight of your brothers and sisters. As the eldest boy you had your hands full, this time with Aidan the youngest of the fourteen kids – and they were tough times in the Dublin tenements.

It was a time for decision. You were expelled from school a couple of years ago but in that serious recession you got a job. The Ma was determined you continue your education at night school which was happening. But night school interferes with your training for soccer fame.

But you don't need my advice Liam because you had the Ma kicking ass. She always said you had to take responsibility for your own future and football ends at 30 so forget about playing for Manchester United. Keep on training for fitness and health but focus on getting your own business up and running

You have the street smarts. You are a quick thinker and no one can keep up with your willingness and ability to multi task. But it's great to add some academic achievements to that list. With that combination you can aim for the stars because there is nothing you can't do.

Liam, did you ever dream you would have a multimillion business empire? Did you ever dream you would be a big TV star? Did you ever dream you would dine with Presidents in the White House, and with royalty in Buckingham Palace? Yes, of course you did and you worked your butt off and made those dreams come true.

But now I am giving you something you never thought too much about back then. You are going to make it as "The First Irishman in Space" one day. Just like Buck Rogers and Dan Dare – Pilot of the Future. So why not? The Ma's voice is still telling you there's nothing you can't do. Go for it and make it happen.

Bill Cullen
(Liam as a kid)

Dustin Enterprises Europe INC
PO BOX 123, Sallynoggin

30/06/10

Dear Meself!

How the divil are ya me ol' pal???!!!

Right so, when I was first asked to write a letter to me 16-year-old self I said "How much?", then the lad on the phone said "One page" – he wasn't from round these parts so I explained to him that I meant how much would me fee be for undertaking such a task. He then told me there wouldn't be a fee, then we got "cut off". A few minutes later the lad rings me back and explained that it was a fundraiser for The Irish Youth Foundation so I says fair enough, once I don't have to meet that clown Bill Cullen wot runs the gaff I'd consider doing me bit. Waffling on about the idea, he was tellin' me that I'd be writing a letter back in time to my 16-year-old self. It was then I told him I was only 12 and that in my 20-plus years as a national icon I'd never been approached by someone who knew so little about me. He then went on about all the other megastars that have done these letters – turns out some of the planet's finest spoofers (Elton John, Jonathan Ross and me ex, Patsy Kensit) were past letter writers so I knew I'd be following in good footsteps, and despite the amateur nature of the approach I've decided to go ahead and dictate (I don't do writing, can't with me wings) a letter to me 16-year-old self.

Dustin Enterprises Europe INC LTD PLC
PO BOX 123, Sallynoggin, Dublin.

First up, I'd advise meself to use me immense talents wisely - at 16 I'll probably be pretty much a global sex symbol/ superstar but it's important to remember that with such talent comes great responsibility... just because motts like Grainne Seoige, Britney Spears and Bibi Baskin will be throwing themselves at me it's crucial to remember that they are people too, complete with feelings and emotions and that I should treat them with the respect they deserve... even the ginger lad Bibi. I'd also remind myself that RTE is essentially just a home for beardy tank-top-wearing fools and just because they weren't smart enough to give ya the Late Late gig when The Plank "decided" to move on it doesn't mean that you're not the greatest broadcaster this country has ever produced - you are, well you and Michael Ryan from Nationwide, who we all know is the King of Irish TV.

Also Dustin, don't be so hard on Ray D'Arcy for leggin' it on you and Socky to make his millions on Today FM, as you'll find out it wasn't just about the money, he just couldn't stay on in RTE after being caught in the stationery cupboard with Shirley Temple Bar... so, so sad - they were set to be one of our nation's leading celebrity couples before that dark day in Montrose.

So Dusty, stay true to your genius and always wash your giblets... and remember that Late Late gig will be yours in good time, there's no way The Twig Tubridy will last, the people of Eire won't stand for it, he WILL be moved on.

GO ON YA GOOD THING!!!!!

Dustin! 4x4

Wicklow
July 2010

Dearest,
    You are doing great! Keep on enjoying school. It's true they are the best years + I'm so glad you are having such fun. Being an Eccles Street girl is a terrific start in Life

    Stop fretting about maths. You are _not_ a dunce. You'll never need them except when a couple of dodgy accountants you'll encounter pull a fast one on you. But don't worry about that either— 'what we put into the lives of others comes back into our own' —that's an Edward Markham quote — its one of the guidelines we use, you + I, in how we live our life.

    Keep questioning always. You are spot on about religion. Most religions are a tool of the Patriarchy to keep women suppressed, + to control the Masses. Go within + find your true Spirit where there is infinite wisdom, love + equality that connects us to each other. We are all equal — Well done for sussing that out so soon.

    Keep enjoying our gorgeous family. You will find that they + good friends are all that really matter. Cherish every hug you get from our wonderful parents. Their love will fortify you in difficult times. Stay close to Mary & the lads, they are the best.

Keep writing those essays! Your vivid imagination will lead you on a wonderful path.

If — sorry — when a gorgeous engineering student with the initials LD asks you out — go!. Be wary of 'Poor me' charmers with brown eyes. You are right about one thing — humour & kindness are the traits to go for in a boy & in a man.

This is turning into a Novel (that's a hint)

Just keep enjoying your life & having fun & trust that all that is for you won't pass you by.

Lots of love
Tricia xxx

P.S. Never ever invest your hard earned money in bank shares & avoid a bank called Anglo like the Plague.

27th July '10

DEAR VICTORIA

Darling heart I know you are livid. And crushed with guilt, but it was nothing to do with you. I promise. Families don't collapse because the eldest child is on a French exchange. Parents split for a host of reasons that I will talk you through when you are old enough to comprehend the grand spectrum of desire and disappointment.

So jettison the guilt. Do you really think if you had been at home and not learning how to say 'I don't eat horse' to your host family in Lyon, France, that your powers of persuasion would have salvaged your cozy nest? No Vic, not a chance. C'est la vie.

I am you, you are me. I am writing to you with the knowledge gleaned from having simply made it to our mid thirties. We now have a handsome husband, 3 creative and happy kids and a career as an actress. Seems almost impossible to you now I bet: The idea that marriage will be something you will believe in, let alone do. Laugh that bitter, hardened laugh freely, Sweet One, as it will be your sound track for our 16th year.

I suggest for the time being that you keep playing the role of Angry Clown at school. It's working for you, attempting to manage the constant indigestion of agony. That acidic eddy living in your gut is just pain. First pain. The last 15 years have been idyllic and that is why it feels so overwhelming, Vic. Why you secretly believe it's your fault. It must be, because Mum and Dad are wonderful. It can't be them. Or your brother, he is super smart and kind (not to mention permanently attached to his Amiga computer). It must be you! You are useless, you reckon.

I promise my lovely, you are not. You simply hurt.

So keep mocking yourself, ya big ginger-afro paddy. Persist in entertaining your posh new friends in the fancy English school you now go to. For the time being anyway. There will come a time where batting off emotion and failure with a trite 'but I cant! I come from a broken home!' will deaden.
Now that I have an email address for you, I will tell you when to stop and maybe you can avoid the leaden heart I carried for a time.

Not sure if this has happened for you yet but two outlets for your rage are on their way Vic. Mum going to bring home a punch bag for physical venting (Oh soo wonderful to kick something that cant get you back) and a teacher will arrive this year. Her name is Miss Sacre. Keep an eye out for her. She is a proud lesbian in short picture socks, who will have about herself a world of possibilities to add to your rarefied school air.

Theatre studies. Sounds like another cop out class akin to typing for GCSE level doesn't it? Trust me, the ability to touch type will come in very handy as, twenty years on, the world will render writing with implements dead (crazy!). As for theatre studies, well, it is to become your future if you want it.

Between you and me, Miss Sacre thinks you live in a caravan outside the home county borders and are on scholarship. Let her. It takes nothing from you. She is making a red haired, Irish, assumption. She will harness your anguish and use it for drama. It will light an ambition within you and give you a way to emote that is legit. One day Miss Sacre will realize you come from a successful family, a glorious, warm home. She'll struggle to equate a straight talking, emotionally raw, ginger fighter, with a home the Duchess of York will eventually buy when the divorce ink is dry. Ha! How lucky you are.

You are.

This pain will subside. You won't be 16 forever.
The spots will fade eventually, so stop putting toothpaste on them.
Don't dye your hair.
Try not to beat yourself up, believe in yourself, and in your brother. He will marry well and have a son in his image.
Your parents haven't divorced you or Dermot. Only themselves.
Years from now, they will get on great. One is married with kids and the other is happily dating a hottie in Monaco. However, I still get nervous when they are together at functions. You know why? I never let it go enough when I was 16. So, do me, us, a favor, Vic's. Let it go. Mum and Dad are not yours to control, just yours to love. As they do you and Derm.

Victoria
AGED 30 SOMETHING AND A HALF

Ps. ...still haven't eaten horse....xx

Kevin Myers

Dear Kevin,

This is the darkest hour of your life, I know. Dad dropped dead a few weeks ago, intestate, and Mum has no money, and I'm sorry to say, things will continue to deteriorate. For soon you will all have to move out of the family home where you were raised and into something more modest, and poor Mum will take in paying guests to get by.

You'll do OK at your O-levels in a couple of months, and you'll start doing A-levels in Chemistry, Biology and Physics. You're doing this because you want to follow in Dad's footsteps as a doctor. This is a mistake, as you will later discover. But you're too grief-stricken to study, and too sunk in the confusion of adolescence to realise very much.

You will fail all of your A-levels, Kevin, the lot. Everyone you know will depart to university. Next you will study fresh A-levels at a third rate tech in Leicester, living with your mother and the paying guests. It seems terrible, because it is terrible. Your next A-level results will be catastrophic – far too poor to qualify you for anything. And this confirms what you already know: You Are a Failure.

Listen, Kevin. CONCEDE NOTHING TO THAT BASE GOD, FAILURE. In all Adversity, you must rise from the floor. But remember – when you do rise, Adversity will certainly respond by striking you again. That's its way. So you must rise again. As long as Adversity is standing over you, you must always rise. You must make that your way.

You always put great outward store in your English public school on your Irishness. If you show that Irishness in the coming years, the base god Failure need not await you, but instead you will find its great and deadly foe, True Happiness.

But that can only happen if you attend to your duties, work hard, and be decent to people, whether you think they deserve or it or not. You must try to tell yourself the whole truth before you try to tell any of it to others, and most of all, you must always reject the siren call of Failure. ALWAYS ALWAYS ALWAYS.

I know you have one really big question. Your endless interest in women: when does it go away?

Sorry, lad: can't help you there.

Kevin

DEREK LANDY

this is what you're going to look like aged 35 ←

Hello me,

Let's see, you're 16, right? So that would make it 1990 when you're reading this. Wow. You haven't even seen Terminator 2 or Silence of the Lambs yet. Do you know what a mobile phone is? Has the internet been born?

I don't have an awful lot of space here, so I'm going to give you five pieces of advice to help guide you through the next, oh, twenty years or so. Pay attention now, I know how easily your mind can wander.

Important! →

1. Dreamers who succeed are lauded for their perseverance. Dreamers who fail are condemned for their delusions. Do not fail.

I know you haven't a clue what you're going to do with your life, aside from some vague idea that you want to be an artist or a writer. Can I be honest? You're not cut out to be an artist. Also, um, you're going to get kicked out of art college and spend the next ten years working on the family farm. But don't despair! It'll work out! I

② You should at least PRETEND to worry about your future every now and again. I think it'd reassure Mum that you're, y'know, capable of taking something seriously.

③ Embrace arrogance. It's much funnier than humility.

As a writer, you're going to get a few knocks. Not everyone is going to recognise your mind-blowing talent straight away, so you'll have to build up a wall of ego to see you through the tough times.

And once the tough times are over, let your ego grow to previously unheard of proportions. It really annoys your friends.

Sage Piece of advice, This.

Me in a Car

Aalii! Nwrba!

4. Be prepared for the fact that you're _never_ going to grow up.

Impressively, you manage to make it in life despite being physically incapable of assuming any responsibility whatsoever. In twenty years time, most of your friends are married with kids. They spend their money on practical things. You spend your money on toys and lightsabers. Enjoy who you are. I know I am.

Lightsaber —>

5— This last one's a four-tiered piece of advice:

A. Ask Catherine out again. Third time's the charm.

B. New Year's Eve 1995— take that chance. You will NOT regret it. (That's a complete lie— you WILL regret it, but not for a year or so.)

C. Appreciate Angie when you have her.

D. Women will torment your life. They're what make it f

...that, my young handsome friend, is that. You have a lot to look forward to. Civilisation is but a few years away— a world of mobile phones, Google, iTunes, DVDs, and Jessica Alba. Also, by the time you reach 33, you will start to age backwards.

And as a parting gift, I just want to say something, something that you actually already know:

You really ARE as cool as you think you are.

We rock!

Smell you later!

Derek

Edmonton Canada 1978 Having a break with my teammates !!.

Hi Barry,

You have just won the Irish title at your third attempt, congratulations. It was hard work wasn't it!! Well you're going to have to work even harder to step up to the next level.

You are about to leave school, I know you're not happy about it but you're making the right decision. It's impossible to train twice a day, help Mum in the shop and do your school work but don't be too concerned, your love of reading is a big help.

Always see the good in people but don't trust everybody because as Dad is always telling you, "in life many people will let you down" and as ever he's right.
Try to spend more time with Dad and your brother Dermot. Tell Dermot how much he means to you, it's important.

In a couple of years from now you'll be encouraged by "someone" to perm your hair, for God sake resist at all costs!

Oh yeah, that beautiful girl across the road that you have been mad about for years, she just might be more interested in you than you think at the moment, so don't give up.

Barry I can't begin to tell you how many exciting and sometimes despairing times lie ahead for you in the coming years, it really is something, so tuck up and roll with the punches.

Cheers

Hi Patrick,

(I've put 'Hi' Instead of 'Dear', cos its less formal and I sound less like your bank manager or Gran-mother.).

Your probably thinking 'how do I know your name, when we've never met?'

I see you buying all that Vinyl at the age of 16 thinking, "Wow this is an investment - Cutting edge music on 12 inch Vinyl, no one will have a collection like this!" Well, there's a few car boot sales every weekend with Stalls full of adults trying to sell there dream collection for 20p a pop.

Remember those thoughts you've had while stood all summer inside the Quorn factory packing sausages and burgers into boxes and onto pallets, from 6am to 2pm, 6days a week at £4 an hour - taking over £30 a day home thinking " Wow I can't wait till I'm a proper grown adult earning this kind of cash every day, I'll be minted! I can't wait to own me own house, have me own mortgage, have me own bills, have me own council tax, have me own water rates, have me own heating bills! What a laugh, I can't wait for it! "

Remember as you munch down 7 'Jaffa Cakes' in a row, savour the flavour! Never checking the 'nutritional 'information' or ingredients, not even wanting to know how many carbohydrates or what percentage of the fat is saturated fat, and how many of your daily allowance of calories it covers! Or how much sugar content per biscuit? Or worry about whether 'a jaffa Cake' is a biscuit or a cake? Instead of just eating it!

Remember sat with dad watching Dave Allen (the 9 & ½ fingered comedian) on telly, thinking "wow how funny is that bloke, just sat there in a chair with a glass of water & he can talk for ages and recite funny stories, just sipping water! And then you'd be in the local pub seeing blokes sat by the bar all night trying to recite stories as funny as Dave Allen, but if only there glasses where full of more water and less beer they may have been able to get some of the stories out right and in half the time!

Remember when we locked our art teacher in the cupboard and we all laughed all summer! Well I've now stopped laughing at that, and I'm actually panicking quite a bit, cos I'm not sure if he was ever let out?

Rember your mum waiting for you to come home every night! And you saying "I'm 16 years old mum I'm not a kid anymore!" Well now adays I hate not being a kid and I have to wait for mum to come home!

All I say is keep on living care free and keep making those simple little memories that you think you may one day forget and be long forgotten! Don't worry, I'll keep them memories safe for you and only pull them out and stare at them when I want to have a break from adulthood and maturity!

Your Best Mate and Secret Keeper

Patrick Monahan

mittens 🐾🐾
H.Q
Dublin
2010

Dear Me,

Keep the fire, no matter what, however small.
That's what lights the bonfires. And they're really worth waiting for.

Don't be afraid of the dark,
that's where you'll find your bearings when your eyes adjust

to the light.

Show love everyday, at least once.
Make sure you accept love everyday,
so don't miss it when it meets you.

Listen to and enjoy the things you want on the road,
but walk in the direction of what you need.

Relish the journey.
Relish the sparkle.
Sparkle.

Love Julie Feeney.

Ray   Foley

Antone, Dublin
1st August 2010

Dear 16-year-old me,

Please get a haircut and stand up straight! Believe me, you will spend years alone if you don't. Be confident - you'll never look this good again - although you'll spend years and a fortune trying. Exercise more now. I'm very unfit.

I'm writing this one month before your/my 3rd birthday - good news! you're still alive ... and married! I think you're really gonna like her. She's WAY out of your league! You won't like reading this, but your father was/is right! You can't please all of the people all of the time - so you should spend less time trying. Enjoy life more, and think less about what other people think. You'll squander your 20's if you don't ... and you'll regret that.

[To Do]
= Save
• Eat less carbs
• Meet girls
• Do J1
• Finish colleg
• Travel
• Chill
• Buy Apple shares
• Avoid Eircom shares
• Copyright "Harry Potter"
• Play Lotto

31/7/2010

Numbers:

10 — Don't worry - you don't have any kids yet - but your wife is extremely demanding. Please learn how to drive

21 — next year - the bus is a pain in the arse for ten years, and you'll pass your test first time! It's easy!

29 — Do not get a credit card, and start saving now if you want to buy a house. But wait

38 — Start saving now if you want to spend it - RECESSION!

42 — until 2010 before you spend it - RECESSION!

44 — Stop thinking about radio and start thinking more about girls - good news! They'll

€2.7 million!

• Watch Lost Start thinking more about girls - good news! They'll to making movies of The Lord of The Rings, a

• Seriously, chill out. spiderman trilogy and Iron man in years to come. Batman goes down-hill but restarts again in 2005... I'm beginning to see why you were single all those years...

Ray Foley (future you)

Dear Me

It's your older self here at 52. Believe it or not, there is life beyond 20. I'm very happy at the moment but I won't tell you too much, it would spoil the surprise. Just a few words of advice.

Enjoy the moment. Enjoy the journey you are on and try not to think too far into the future. Things don't always turn out the way you expect but don't be disappointed. There can be great fun in the unexpected. Actually sometimes it turns out to be better than the expected. Try to live in the moment as much as possible... that's where happiness is.

The most important thing in life is people but there are different types. As your good friend Molly told you, there are givers and there are takers. Look out for the takers. When you find the good ones, hold on to them, treasure them. But do try to look for the good in everyone...it's there and it's worth finding.

I suppose above all don't worry. You are going to have a great life. (Until 52 anyway, I can't vouch for it after that.) Oh yeah, if you do come across a horse called Red Rum or Istabracq, put a few pounds on them.

Take Care,

Michael 'Sue' O'Sullivan, Gerard Murphy, Ray Styles and Rob Davis of Mud, Kevin Sheehy,
Mike 'Tuas' O' Sullivan, Jon Kenny and Eugene O'Sullivan at the launch of their single
'Laugh, Live and Love' at the Chariot Inn, Dublin in 1977.

Apartment 1.746,
Rosa Parks (Cube 3, South Quarter),
Ticknock,
(I can't Believe It's Still) Dublin.

Dear Ross,

First of all— and I know this is going to sound big-headed— but let me just say how well you're looking at the moment. Get used to it! Those looks are going nowhere! As far as everything else goes ...

Okay, here it is. You are going to grow up to be one of the best Rugby players, not only in Ireland, but in, like, the World? You are going to score more tries for this country than any player in history, including a hat-trick in Paris at the age of, like, 21. You will captain Ireland to a first Grand Slam since 1948. You will also captain the Lions, marry a beautiful actress and become a Source of happiness and hope for people during what will be the worst period of, like, Recession in the Country's history. Yes, it's all ahead of you. All you have to do is this one thing...

There's a dude called Brian O'Driscoll. He's, like, the same age as you and he plays for, like, Blackrock College. First opportunity you get, spear-tackle him. It will Save you a whole lot of pain. Trust me.

Ross

© Alan Clarke

Rathmines, D6
July 2010

Dear Ardal,

In response to your rather alarming note I'll try and explain briefly why life, your life, is in fact worth living.

Firstly, since I'm pretty sure this is what's eating you, that mysterious girl you met during the holidays still likes you. Yes, even now! Okay, she still has the faraway look and the hacksaw tongue but, my, she's burgeoned into a pretty comprehensive woman — beautiful, bursting with life, and just. She's been the one comfort in an irremediable world. A selfless companion and ultramother fair!

So forgive me if I tell you that the fatalism is trying, a bit one-note. And the poetry is a bit trite. Time doesn't drag. Well, not always. For the past 20 years, it's been a blitzkrieg of ambition fulfilled & wildest dreams realised. Even the darkest days sing with the chatter of happy children.

What else? (I know you want to get back to your Somerset Maugham!) Oh yes! You won't believe this. The urban guerilla war in the North is over! I'm serious. There are ongoing problems but the peace has pretty much held since 1998. And, if that doesn't cheer you up, Ireland has qualified for one European championship & three World Cups! You see, it's not 'mental' to hope.

AOH

In Conclusion, my advice to you is to stop behaving like some careworn Victorian consumptive and arise from the chaise longue. Eat more fruit! Be taller! The world is scary, for sure, but also a thrilling place.

Yours sincerely
Ardal (44)

Damien Dempsey

Dear young fella,

Please, I implore you to use your guitar for firewood and get a trade. If you stick at music you'll drink buckets of Guinness and eat many many burgers for twenty years until you're eventually twenty-five stone and have to do lunchtime gigs in Supermacs just to clear your slate – just kidding, but only just.

I know you're a bit angry and bewildered by your mother leaving home this year but deep down you know they should have split a long time ago, married too young like so many Irish people of their church/neighbour-fearing generation. (Remember your Uncle Mihal saying that if you saw a girl's ankle you had to marry her?) Just realise that your mother has great courage to leave, divorce is still illegal in Ireland and she is the first person on your street of seventy houses to have the balls to leave a failing marriage. Don't feel ashamed by your parents splitting up because although it's not the norm in this country now, some day soon it will be quite a common occurrence, just as it was in the days of the Brehon Laws in your country before Roman Catholic and English colonisation.

You'll come second in the 2FM national song contest this year with your song about the homeless, 'Cardboard City'. I know that ghetto blaster you win gives you dreams of the stage and your name in lights and all that jazz, but just realise if you do take the music route, which of course is mandatory as music is like oxygen to you by now, don't lose faith. If you could see the people you're going to sing and record and perform with and the venues you'll play around the world you'd quit school now – but don't do that either, because it's all part of the journey and you're leaving next year anyway.

Many times over the next penny-pinching decade you're gonna ask yourself why you went with the music and lots of people will tell you you're flogging a dead horse, it's going to be a long, oft-times disheartening, struggle I'm afraid, young brother. Critics in papers and on the street will try to tear you asunder but roll with their spineless punches and some day you'll sing with all your living heroes. It'll be nearly ten years before you're able to release an album, you'll come in for a lot of bigotry for singing reggae-tinged urban Irish folk in a working-class accent, but hang on in there (you stubborn little bollix) through the hard penniless times when you feel like quitting and some day many will come around. You'll even make working-class people with low self-esteem feel more pride, and you'll bring hope and joy and some little known history to people from all walks of life with your music, and get them singing at the gigs like there's no tomorrow.

As with many kids in the neighbourhood I know you've been dabbling in the drink and drugs these past few years but the few fights you'll have this year in the boxing will keep you from going doolalley on them and you haven't the money to go too nuts anyway unless you started selling them and we both know that's not you. They will result in you getting bouts of bad depression over the next few years but you'll come through that by knocking them on the head and getting into meditation and swimming. And try not to be as quick with your fists with street bullies when you're drinking; I know you got sick of their shit and started to lash out but you're not like them and you have a bit of respect now. If you feel a situation coming on get the hell outta there; there's a lot tougher and more vicious than you out there and your friends and family need you. And remember, you're a musician, you're posh now.

Over the next few years you'll do five months labouring through an Irish winter, which will give you great respect for those who do heavy manual work for a living, you'll barback in a New York Irish bar called Rocky's and double up as bouncer when needed. You'll do a Community Employment Scheme (when you're cut off welfare) in Finglas doing songwriting workshops for two years with disadvantaged kids and see their amazing talent that when harnessed properly is so powerful, it will all be great experience for your writing.

Anyway try and keep the drink a bit moderate, keep up the sea swimming, jogging and boxing training, do a bit of yoga and meditation, realise creative people can be prone to depression so keep the chin up through the dark times and remember your positive lyrics when you need to, if you don't you can't expect anyone else to. Love yourself today young brother and see you in nineteen years.

xx

Damien

Ian Dempsey

Dear Ian,

I hope you don't mind me saying this, but have you noticed that your belly is getting a bit bigger? Maybe you should lay off the spiceburgers and the bottles of beer before it's too late – and I know you're not very sporting, but you should take a bit of exercise. You'll never be Eamon Coughlan but you should at least try or you could end up being the next Elvis. Very sad.

While I'm at it, all the other lads have girlfriends, how come you're so slow off the mark? Stop letting on that you're not really bothered about it. I mean, that girl you met up near the roundabout – she likes you, you like her – why do you have to be so shaky? How come you turn into a quivering wreck and all the oxygen seems to leave your brain in the presence of a girl? Cop on.

Actually I'm surprised she's even giving you a second look. That gear you wear, I know it's the fashion but it looks a bit odd. A tank top is what I believe they call the top bit. And the trousers are too short – is that what they're supposed to look like? And your hair – does that style have a name? Your Dad reckons you look ridiculous but I think he's given up trying to talk sense into you. Did you ever think that maybe – just maybe – he's right? It wouldn't be the first time.

By the way, have you started studying for the Christmas exams yet? It'll be too late the week after next. I know at your age time goes very slowly and the days are long but things change and in another couple of years you'll be able to spread your wings and travel to somewhere exotic or you could move out and get yourself a flat and become a little more independent. I mean, you don't want to end up staying at home until you get married, do you? Start planning now.

You were saying that music is what you're most interested in so what are you going to do about it? You've tried to learn how to play the piano and failed miserably and now the guitar – same story. Why don't you stick with it and in a few years you'll have cracked it. And this disc jockey business is great fun but you'll never make a career out of being on the radio. You need to listen to your career adviser and maybe take up accountancy or try for the civil service.

One more thing: I know you are hanging on every word that David Bowie says but everybody else thinks he's a weirdo so try to be less fanatical if that's possible. You probably won't even remember his name in ten years' time. Why not try somebody more wholesome – like Johnny Rotten?

Here's to the future.

Ian

2010

David Norris

Dear Me (or indeed, dearie me!),

So I have got to sit right down and write myself a letter. Myself at 16 that is. Well as I am 65 as I write I can see clearly now – so here goes.

Number 1 – highly important! – don't worry about the zits. They'll pass and leave not a trace behind. The same with the hair by the way, it will pass too and leave very little trace except on your behind. But don't worry, that just means you are testosterone-charged, baby.

So basically keep your sense of humour. Laugh at yourself first and others afterwards so that the others will appreciate that you are not just trashing them. Laughter that is not spiteful is good for the body, soul and mind. On top of that, do you want to know a secret? Life gets better all the time. All those little knocks that looked as if they might end your world will be no match for your middle-aged emotional shock absorbers. To continue being prompted by well-loved lyrics, hackneyed but true – "Accentuate the Positive, Eliminate the Negative" and always remember, love is the greatest thing and there really is one for everyone in the audience. What's more, on top of that if you are lucky or greedy a second helping or two is often available as well so keep on sucking diesel.

Love you, dream boat.

You get sexier every day.

David

P.S. On a serious note as Shakespeare said, "To Thine Own Self Be True". It really does liberate you in the end. I instinctively felt that when I was you at the age of 16, and my life since has fully vindicated it. The other critical piece of advice is to tell you how right you were never to let any other individuals or groups have control over your life. Always keep the reins in your own hands.

David **Coleman**

3 August 2010

Dear David,

Having been 16 all those years ago, I understand that by now you do believe that you know it all. However, I feel obliged to share a few tips that I have learned over the years and you can thank me later that you didn't have to learn them the hard way.

1. Women appreciate hygienic men. In this regard you should know that roll-ons are more effective than spray deodorants and a razor blade always shaves closer than an electric razor - just be careful of spots!

2. Life begins a great new stage when you move out of home. The food is good @ home but not that good. Get out and live.

3. Always remember that you are capable and lovable. I know that you are capable of being anything you want to be and I love you; but you need to believe that yourself.

4. Always drive as nice a car as you can afford. Life is too short and driving is too much fun to bother with the dross.

I know these might not, exactly, be words of wisdom but I thought you should know them anyway. Mind yourself,

All my love,

David.

Dear 16 year old me

Wow, this is weird being able to write to you from the future. You look like you're having a good day - class was good, you won your football match and was that you I saw sneaking off hand in hand into the woods?!!!

But don't forget I know you and so I see your down days too - people making jokes about you, about your weight. Being brave at your last two auditions when they shouted "NOT GOOD ENOUGH..... NEXT." You smile through it until nobody is looking.

Let me tell you looking back from the future you are never going to please everybody all of the time so don't let critisism get you down. Push boundaries. Grab opportunities and continue to be a little wild! But NEVER forget who you are. Speak up for those around you when they need your support because so many people will support you through life. Those friends I see with you today will still be with you 25 years later.

I won't tell you what course your life will take but you will be priviliged to see amazing places and meet incredible people. You will learn how small we are in this huge world and it will make you smile. You will laugh loud and often. Most importantly that family who irritate you from time to time, yet who you love, will always be there for you. Life is a long road and you'll get lost sometimes but if you never forget who you are you'll always find your way. Lots of love from yourself xxx

The
E...

Schoolhouse Hotel
★ ★ ★ ★

Dear Sonia, (Age 16)
      You may not believe this but
when you leave Cobh to study at Villanova
University you are about to embark on a
lifetime of travelling the world. Travelling to
races will take up most of your time, but
many places you will only visit once.
      The best advice I can give you
is to keep a diary, even just for short
notes to remind you of the places you
visit and people you meet. Don't just pack
your camera and leave it in your bag
take plenty photo's and save them each
year in a file with your diary.
      As an athlete you will be determined
to work hard and ignore little aches and pains.

Schoolhouse Hotel, 2-8 Northumberland Road, Ballsbridge, Dublin 4, Ireland.
Tel: +353 1 667 5014   Fax: +353 1 667 5015   Email: info@schoolhousehotel.com
www.schoolhousehotel.com

You need to heed these warning signs as early treatment and detection will get you back running and racing even quicker.

You want to avoid lingering injuries and extended running in the pool, it just maintains fitness and keeps the weight off. I know you would rather be running outside.

When you win a race, take your time to appreciate the

moment and acknowledge the achievement to
yourself. The years will fly by and
before you know it you will be facing
retirement while trying to grasp one las[t]
victory. When you glimpse an opportunity,
grab it with both hands, take your
chances and give it everything you've
got. Have fun ... enjoy the ride before it slows down[.]

The LODGE
DOONBEG GOLF CLUB

THE LODGE AT DOONBEG GOLF CLUB
COUNTY CLARE, IRELAND

return address:

tel: 065-905-5600

web: www.doonbeggolfclub.com

fax: 065-905-5247

The LODGE
DOONBEG GOLF CLUB

as it invariably will
long before you want
to step off the
whirlwind life of an
international athlete.

Take Care,
Smile a lot
& Love Life,

Sonia O'Sullivan

Dear Anna,

You are probably around at the basketball courts, practising like mad and promising God that if you score five three-pointers in a row, you will go to two Masses next Sunday.

Keep it up, it will pay off!

You are going to have the strangest, most interesting couple of years. I don't want to tell you the future, but there are big changes coming your way.

You will beat yourself up that you didn't do well in exams, in fact for years you will have) A recurring dream that you are

in your English leaving Cert. Exam, and you are only wearing
a jumper, pants and white socks.
(Chillax (That's a new word)) Don't worry about it, honestly.
You also feel a bit different from everyone else. I can assure
you that everyone in the class feels the same.

Your difference is going to be something quite unusual.

I know this sounds weird but you are going to fall in love with
other interesting, unusual people.
This will be frightening at first, and then it will be the
happiest day of your life.

Keep doing what you are doing.
You will fall in love and out of love. You will break hearts
and have your own smashed. You will find life so much fun,
and a big laugh.

Failure is always an option, because through it you become a
better person.
OK, ENOUGH of the CRAP — GET BACK TO THE GUEST'S,
love
Aunt

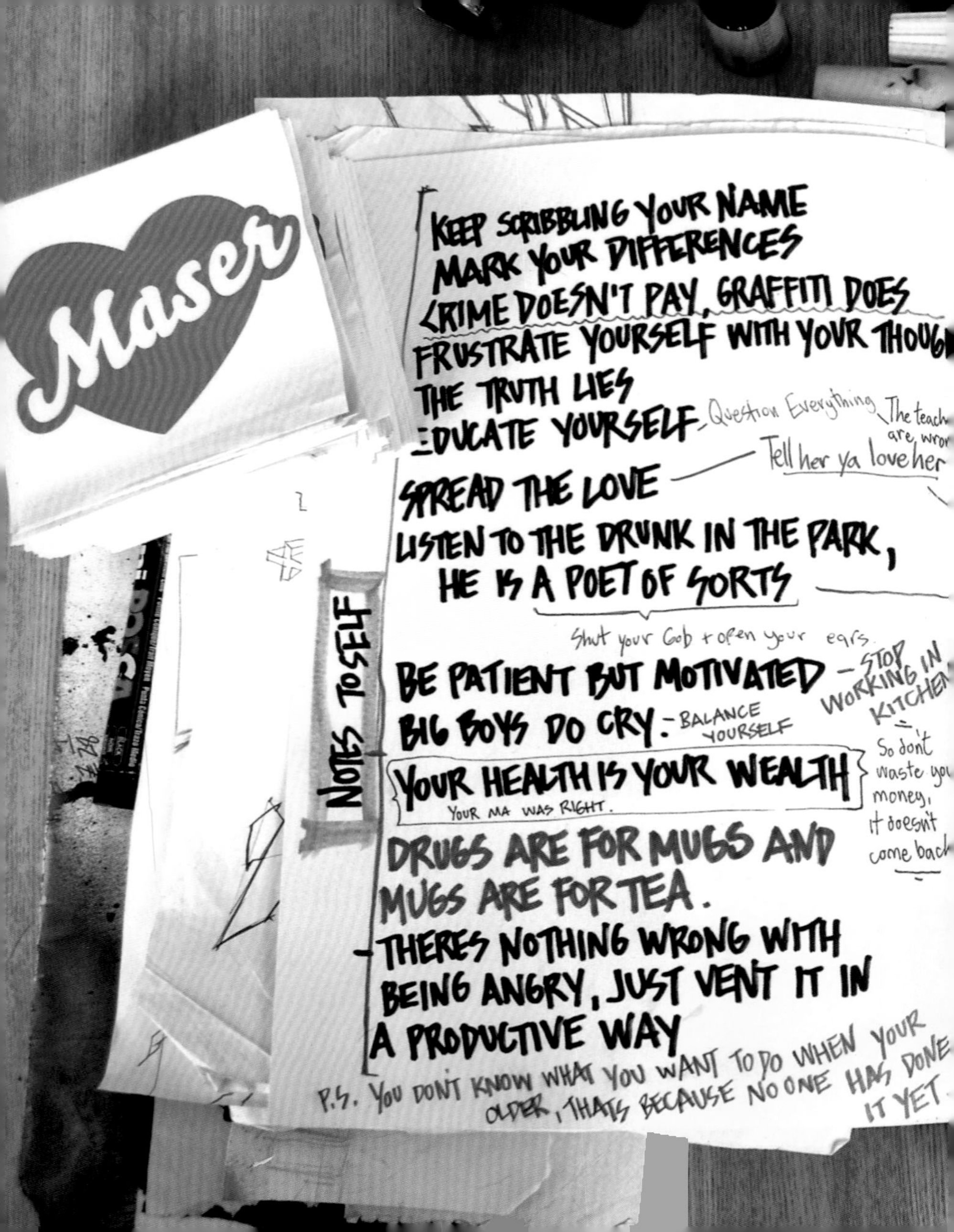
Maser
NOTES TO SELF
KEEP SCRIBBLING YOUR NAME
MARK YOUR DIFFERENCES
CRIME DOESN'T PAY, GRAFFITI DOES
FRUSTRATE YOURSELF WITH YOUR THOUG
THE TRUTH LIES
EDUCATE YOURSELF – Question Everything – The teach are wron
SPREAD THE LOVE – Tell her ya love her
LISTEN TO THE DRUNK IN THE PARK, HE IS A POET OF SORTS
Shut your Gob + open your ears.
BE PATIENT BUT MOTIVATED – STOP WORKING IN KITCHEN
BIG BOYS DO CRY. – BALANCE YOURSELF
YOUR HEALTH IS YOUR WEALTH
YOUR MA WAS RIGHT.
So don't waste you money, it doesn't come bac
DRUGS ARE FOR MUGS AND MUGS ARE FOR TEA.
THERES NOTHING WRONG WITH BEING ANGRY, JUST VENT IT IN A PRODUCTIVE WAY
P.S. YOU DONT KNOW WHAT YOU WANT TO DO WHEN YOUR OLDER, THATS BECAUSE NO ONE HAS DONE IT YET

OPAQUE, OIL-BASE PAINT MARKER

FOR BEST RESULTS:

MOLOTOW 620 PP

maser loves u

maser loves u

School Days aren't
the best days
of your life.

listen to your
ths teacher when
e starts multiplying letters
—Z

now her you care

love

16 08 '02

edding 152 M

THANKS!

John Rocha

Dublin 2010

Dear John,

I have travelled a long way from Hong Kong and now live in Dublin, Ireland, a very beautiful, lush green country. I came here back in the 1980's drawn in by the gifted craftsmen and their indigenous skills that have survived over the centuries. Like my homeland Hong Kong, history and tradition are important here.

The people are wonderful and you now have three amazing Irish-Chinese children.

You need to thank grandmother for passing on her love of sewing and tailoring to me. I am a designer working in fashion among other disciplines.

It seems crazy to say but in a few years time this young Hong Kong boy will be awarded British Designer of the year and more recently honoured with a CBE - Commander of the British Empire from Her Majesty Queen Elizabeth II for my contribution to fashion. It is a great disappointment dad will not be around to see it.

My advice to you is to grow your hair long like dad and Victor be happy, and enjoy life.

Young John, you will be pleased to hear you are a very lucky man.......

Much love,

John

Dear Cathy,

I must seem ancient to you. Forty-four. That's like a thousand in teenage years.

Right now, you think older people know nothing despite their loud insistence that they know it all. You're quite sure you know nothing, although you desperately wish you did. You've got your head stuck constantly in a book in the hope of learning how to live.

And you're scared.

It seems easier to put on a façade of confidence than to reveal your true self. OK, first bit of advice: facades crumble and ultimately, they hurt you. Be your authentic self.

Your authentic self knows a lot more than you realise. Your instincts are so wise. I wish you'd listen to them.

Say what you think.

Ask questions. It's OK not to know something. Clever people know things because they ask questions.

Don't let anyone put you down. They don't have the right to do that.

You're not ugly or hideous, by the way.

Stand up for other people when they are being bullied or hurt.

Do not be dragged along with the crowd. You are not a crowd person.

You do not need to hang around with crazy cool people to seem interesting. You can be interesting all on your own and in your own way.

Be yourself. Trust me, it will be a lot easier if you do, and I know what I'm talking about,

With so much love

your older self,

Catty xxx

Tony Griffin

Dear 16-year-old Tony Griffin,

I am the 29-year-old you and I am sitting overlooking Lough Derg early on this the last day of June 2010. I wanted to take this time and write to you to tell you some very special things I want you to know. The reason I want you to know is that now when you read this, Tony, you can incorporate what I have learned in your life and so learn to squeeze every last drop out of life.

Firstly, I love you. You are absolutely fantastic. You are courageous, kind, hard-working and a fine athlete. I'll tell you later some of the wonderful things you are going to do, but first I want you to know that where you are right now, you are enough. Believe this, that you are all I say you are and do not doubt yourself. I believe in you.

At the moment you are trying to break on to the Clare under-18 team. You wonder at times "do I have what it takes to play for Clare?" I want to tell you the first of the great things you will go on to do. Here it comes... you will go on to play for Clare, making your debut in 2002. On your debut you will score 0–6 from play, the final point of which will be set up by your hero, Jamesie O'Connor. You will be nominated that year for an All-Star. It gets better – you will play in the All-Ireland final and while you are beaten, you will learn from it. I know at the moment you are conscious of being as thin as a rake, but don't worry, you will go on to transform your body and would you believe it, you will win an All-Star in 2006... yes, it's true. Tony, your greatest challenge will be separating You the person from You the hurler. So now, learn that a bad game does not mean a weak Tony Griffin. On the contrary, you are braver than you realise.

Tony, the second thing I would like to say to you is to just trust the journey, everything will work out as it is supposed to. Daddy will pass away in 2005 and, while you struggle to come to terms with this, you will cycle a bicycle 7000 kilometres across Canada and Ireland and meet Lance Armstrong along the way. All the time you will be guided, so remember: Faith is more powerful than Fear.

And here is a good one for you... on the last day of that 7000-kilometre cycle with just 25 kilometres to go you will meet a girl who you fall in love with. Yes... you. As I write this to you three years after you met her it just gets better and better... trust that as well, like everything else that will go just where it needs to go.

One last nugget for you. You know all those diaries you keep and soul-searching you do? In 2010 you will write a book called 'Screaming at the Sky' – it will go on to be a bestseller and the writing of it will be a wonderful experience. That's our secret.

So as I leave you, Tony, I want to leave you with this. If you knew who walks beside you on this path that you have chosen you would never know fear or doubt again. And Tony, most of all please do not take yourself or life so seriously, learn to smile and laugh at yourself.

With much respect for you.

Love, your 29-year-old self

P.S. Always remember you can achieve ANYTHING you set your mind to and are willing to believe in and work hard for.

Richard Corrigan

August 2010

Hello Richard,

You'll be well and truly shocked to get this letter from me, or should I say from you?

It's amazing but true that I'm writing to you from the future… your future. I know it's hard to believe, but lots of things that seemed impossible dreams in 1980 have come true for you.

I know every single one of your little secrets and dreams because they were OURS. You really should never have had that long hair and thought you were a biker – luckily you grew out of that phase and you still have a good head of hair, just shot through with a bit of grey now. You're a grown man now but still full of devilment, and as argumentative as ever. Some people will call you a contrary bugger – hard to argue with that, but you won't change.

Slipping away to drink that treasured, stolen bottle of Guinness every time Dad killed a pig, I still wonder if he ever knew? You will still be enjoying a pint of Guinness when you're forty-six and will always remember those days, feeding the poor old pig his last apple. Pigs run and hide when they see you coming now.

Life has been good to you so don't worry too much.

Bunking off school so that you could go and work in the kitchens of The Kirwan Arms with Ray Vaughan was the best thing you ever did in your life, it gave you something to hold on to for ever that no schoolroom could have ever given you.

Just to keep you happy I'd better tell you that, unlike most people, you will get to do the one thing in life you always wanted to do –COOK. It took you a good few years to get there (or here) with lots of tough times on the way. You will have more jobs than most people have had hot dinners and for a while you'll be like a 'flying chef' but you're only looking for a good place to land. You will travel all over the world and meet some truly great people and a good few 'chancers', you'll learn a lot about other lives but Ireland will still always be home to you, you will have some amazing times but I'd best not tell you about them…don't want to scare you or ruin any surprises for you.

Oh, and you will get married to a lovely girl and have kids…I won't tell you how many.

You'll make lots of mistakes on the way, and be a right eejit now and again – none of that will mean much though.

You have so much to look forward to, the world has moved on at a ferocious lick, new technology has changed everything (you won't know what that is!). Would you believe that chefs are now celebrities? Some even have their own TV shows, ridiculous eh?

I'd like to give you the winners of a few Grand Nationals but I can't be bothered, you'd only forget to have a bet anyway and you've never liked to have things too easy. Best for you to find your own way.

Just two small tips though: don't buy any shares in Betamax and don't take a job at Hackney Greyhound Track!

Be happy.

From an older, tiny bit wiser, you.

Richard Corrigan

Howya Ray, Hope all is well. I'm not great at this letter writing lark, but here goes.

You know this already because you've been told it by your mother on numerous occasions, You WORRY too much. Relax. Try not to worry about the things you can't change and only worry about the other things when you really have to.

Always do your best at whatever you're doing and try not to have one eye on the next project. In dealing with people be respectful of authority but always be aware of your worth. Remember your opinion is important too. In relationships be honest with yourself, honesty towards others will follow. Have the craic and celebrate achievement. Read more, learn to swim as soon as you can and never pass up the opportunity to be near the sea. Oh and finally your hair isn't as important as you now think! Good luck! Ray

July 27, 2010

Dear Síle,

If your father hits your mother, tell him you don't like it. get your sisters and brothers to join with you in that conversation. Grab what joy you can from your young life, Síle is my now full of that thick excitement of growing up sexually. Do not do anything sexually that does not please you. If you don't want to, say no. Keep dancing. You know by now that Gael Céilí dancing is great — they make everybody take to the floor and it doesn't matter if you're with a female or a male. Stop the smoking now and save up the money for foreign travel. The minute you leave this island, you will be free, out of the house, away from the family. Fly away once in a while.

Nell

Jason Sherlock

Dear Jay, or 'Jayo' as you will have to get used to being called by most of the country!

I will cut to the chase and talk about sport: I know that's all you care about and you will be glad to know that doesn't change, although you may lose perspective along the way.

Firstly basketball: I know you love the game and part of you thinks going to high school in America would be great, but America is a long way from home and there will be amazing opportunities in other sports to come your way. I hate to break it to you but you are 5'7" and will always be 5'7" so the dream of playing in the NBA is very unlikely!

You need to have a think about how much you really care about soccer. You will actually play against the team you support, Liverpool, in Lansdowne Road and after the game their manager will ask you if you would like to go over on trial! I don't want to tell you what to do but one bit of advice I would give you is to go with your gut instinct. That's what I did and it opened me up to an amazing sporting career.

I don't want to tell you everything but you will achieve your dream of playing for Dublin. Along the way you will be well known and be successful but there will also be some difficult times and some heavy defeats. You will be tested as a footballer and a person to overcome these things and if you hang in there it will be all worth it in the end.

Dear Tom,

Chin up, I know you're prone to over analysis and listening morosely and repeatedly to your copy of Bob Dylan's More Greatest Hits, but if you think you have anything to worry about now, you should see what's coming down the line –SCARY!

I am the voice of Future Tom. The fact that you have a future at all might come as a surprise to you, and indeed the entire staff of James St. CBS, but you do and if you could do the following things EXACTLY as requested it will a far less painful one than you might otherwise endure.

1. Slip these words into as many songs as you can until people sit up and pay attention: 'Take a Parachute and jump." Don't worry about the other words, something will come to you.
2. Insist on being in a five piece band. The Dublin of your future will be oversubscribed with four piece bands and one in particular will make life uncomfortable for all the others for FOUR, count them, FOUR, decades.
3. Should you find yourself in the public view, and I'm not saying you will, get a haircut. In fact get several haircuts and a tattoo saying 'Big Hair is Bad.'
4. Keep your vinyl albums in mint condition.
5. Buy property, as much as you can, in the mid nineties and sell all of it on Sep 13th 2008.
6. Crossing Crow Street in the Temple Bar Area on April 22nd, 2004, at about 11.54 AM you will feel a strong urge to turn right. Overcome this urge and turn left. Keep walking and never look back. This is a pivotal moment in your life
7. Read point 6 again
8. and again
9. and again.
10. Never use the word Dude in conversation.
11. You don't look good in check, trust me.

Follow this advice to the letter and your life will fine. In reality, it will all be fine, although I know from talking to you that there is no talking to you. You are in truth a nice kid, although it would kill you to admit that the two people downstairs have actually done a good job on you.

On that point, and I hate to say this, but they really do know what you're up to up there in your room alone. Mortifyingly embarrassing as it is to think, they have actually lived a bit themselves you know. And you aren't the first teenage boy to this, so relax.

Final piece of advice: When your dad offers you a cup of tea, as he does every day at 4.00 PM, just once, don't act like the teenager from hell, and accept the offer. Just once, for Future Tom, please.

Tom Dunne

JASON BYRNE

Dear ~~Jason~~ Jay

I know that you would love to be able to write like this now, but don't worry you will be able to in the future, and it will be simpler than you think. Anyway I'm sure that you're looking at your nose in the mirror right now wondering why it's the biggest thing on your face. Well, let me tell you, "straw balls", it will all become good in your twenties and that's when you'll need your face the most, but it will remain bent slightly, and that will help you in your future career.

Now I won't talk to you for too long, as I know your attention span is tiny, and if I know you I'd even say you stopped reading this after the first two lines because there weren't any pictures. Still loving that Tintin collection, I hope?

So, girls. Right now you have a pen-pal in Canada; best to let her go, she'll only arrive back to Ireland and snog Brian. Don't worry, when you look back on her picture she is a hammer compared to the beautiful women you're about to hear about...your first love will be your strongest and most powerful, go with the flow, but not for too long, then leg it. The next will be a lovely actress, blonde and great fun, but she'll ask you to marry her on her twenty-first birthday, say goodbye politely and leave. You'll then meet a girl who looks like you, she's the next powerful love, just let her leave for Australia. Finally you'll meet your wife, and this is where you will have to strap in like being on a rollercoaster, more twists and turns than you'll ever imagine, but as the rollercoaster comes to a halt, you'll have two beautiful children and a friend for life. Of course I haven't filled you in on all the women that will cross your path, but then that would mean you'd know too much, straw balls. In other words your life will heavily revolve around the ladies.

So, time to go back to Tintin, Jay, and your brother Eric is probably still out, so pop on that Lynyrd Skynyrd album that he owns, grab his T-Square and strum your heart out. Oh and by the way, when two nurses come to your house and ask you to MC a gig, that means to host a show, in the local pub, say yes as it will change your life forever.

And last but not least, listen to this sentence and bring it into play for the rest of your life, and things will come to you quicker than they did to me...DON'T SAY "YES" WHEN YOU MEAN "NO"...good luck brother, you're a lovely fella right now with many friends and they all love you, including me.

See ya!

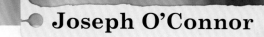

Dear Sixteen-Year-Old Self,

Hi, this is me. This is you plus several decades. Wake up when I'm talking to you! God, look at the state of yourself. What are you like?

Is that an actual hairstyle, or has someone dumped a plate of cold tagliatelle on your head? You look like you slept in a skip.

You're going to have to do something about your appalling diet. It seems to me that you have three criteria for selecting a meal: (A) it must contain monosodium glutamate and saturated fats, (B) it must be capable of preparation by nothing more than the addition of hot water (from the kitchen tap if necessary) and (C) meal consumed, the container in which it was contained has to be capable of being used as an ashtray. Keep eating like this and you're going to be sorry. The day will come, some time in your forties, when you'll realise Tayto cheese-and-onion crisps don't count as a vegetable.

You've never asked me for advice, and you're not asking now. In fact, you wouldn't dream of it; you've never asked anyone, and you'd be embarrassed to be seen even TALKING to me. You think you've all the answers. That's one of the many attractive things about people your age. You think you know everything and you know so little. And I can see you rolling your sixteen-year-old eyes at me as I write you these words. I know your thoughts. You're making them clear. Here's some forty-seven-year-old gobshite getting on my case. Some balding old saddo with blood pressure and a mortgage. You're thinking of The Clash and the Sex Pistols and the Specials, and how they've nothing to say to a middle-aged idiot. Your favourite band, The Who, have a quote for losers like me. 'Things they do look awful cold. Hope I die before I get old.' You might feel like that now. Take it from me, kiddo, that might change.

As for the things you feel about your friends right now, and the things you feel about everyone else your own age: try to get over the desire for everyone to like you. Society inculcates a kind of brutalising need for accomplishment, and in the case of people in their teens this is often how it comes out. But paradoxically, the very minute you give up this desire, the more people want to be friends with you. So be yourself. Don't pretend. Don't fake. There's an idea that people your age are naturally rebellious, but in fact they're intensely conformist and rarely want to differ from one another. Find the courage to differ and you've found what you are. And sometimes have the courage to find yourself strange, while there's still time for you to know yourself at all.

Oscar Wilde said youth is wasted on the young. But he was wrong – old people couldn't handle it. The thing that disappears over the years is time. You'll be working, maybe parenting, the hours turn to minutes, and with a baby in the house, should you ever be so lucky, a lie-in until about 7.30 a.m. gets to feel like a week-end in the country. Oh, and enjoy your Hair, while you've got so much of it. We men get a cruel trick played on us by fate. As we age, the hair on our head recedes in inverse proportion to that growing on other parts of us. The day is going to come when you guiltily find yourself whispering to the barber, 'Take a little off the sides. And then do the ears.'

The sex thing, you're going to have to figure out for yourself. But I do know one thing – you have to make a little effort. The days are gone when the chat-up line 'I own a farm and all my own teeth' really worked. You're going to have to try harder, if you can.

Astonishingly, given your ineptitude and awkwardness and lack of confidence, you're going to one day fall in love and realise you can't be without her. The courage you're going to find, the joy you're going to feel – I wish I could put it into words for you. Since I can't, let me give you a few lines from a little poem I'd like you to rehearse. You're going to find yourself reading them aloud, twenty years from now, to a room full of your wedding guests. It's a translation from Horace, by the Irish poet Derek Mahon. I'm not quoting the lines accurately, I'm quoting from memory. Memory is a kind of imagination. But the thought at the heart of them is still going to come to you, in strange moments of the day, in warm moments and tough ones, when being sixteen seems another country.

Do not waste your time
In fear and hope.
Accept whatever happens.
Ignore
The horoscope.
For the days are more fun than the years.
Which pass us by
While we discuss them.

Lots of love,
Joseph

Dear John,

There's nothing you need less than words of wisdom from the likes of me. As you have long suspected, grown-ups rarely know what they're talking about. The problem of course is that adults are often obliged to give the impression that they do - parents have no choice and teachers get paid for it. So go easy on them. We're all making it up as we go along.

I don't like giving advice in any case and you're not used to getting it, but I'll chance this much even so. Never assume that adults know the score and don't ever take it for granted that they know what's best for you. The chances are that they don't. So you'll just have to follow your instincts. Be confident. Be strong. Be your own man and do your own thing. Learn French.

These are tricky times I know. You're searching for clues and people keep hiding them from you. All you're getting at school is what they call "guidance" and that magazine the priest hands out. *Reality*. An outrageous misnomer if ever there was one. Some of these people mean well, but none of them have any real sense of who you are. I recommend that you read as many novels as you can. Read them twice and three times. That's where the real info is. I could go on. And I often do.

Basically you're on your own, pal. But you're well able for it. Do your own thing and good luck.

John

JOHN KELLY

Dear Me,

I hope you're okay, though I suspect you're not.

I know you're going to find this hard to believe right now, but things actually work out incredibly well. No – you don't end up marrying that really handsome dark haired guy from Trinity who sits upstairs on the 46a bus, so if I was you I'd stop right now bothering to get that same bus home every day from college – trust me, that's an absolute waste of time.

Also, lay off all the swotting a bit – you don't need to get a first, you just need to pass your exams as you don't end up being an academic. In fact, you're not even a lawyer. So chill out and start enjoying yourself.

Also, you should really try and stop being so sad all the time - if it's attention you're looking for, you're wasting your time. In fact, you're just very annoying and deeply self indulgent. The patience of your big sister must be wearing seriously threadbare by now. I mean she's kind enough to keep taking you out with her friends as she knows you're a bit sad and lonely – but crying in the UCD bar in front of her seriously cool college friends – that's just not a good look, believe me.

And since we're on the topic of 'looks' – what's with this eating no food lark? Honestly – being five foot ten and a half inches and weighing seven stone isn't sexy – not even one teeny teeny bit. In fact, I can tell you now, in all honesty, that you look woegeous – no sensible guy would fancy you in a trillion years. So start eating, for goodness sake. You're going to look so much better when you put on a bit of weight – you just think you're fat because you have what they now call 'self esteem issues'. Too boring to go into right now, believe me.

Also, you know the way you walk around college all day lonely and hardly speak to anyone, except your dear friend from school Maria – has it ever entered your head that you could come across as a tad stand offish?

I probably sound a bit harsh right now, because I know you are truly sad a lot of the time and do often cry yourself to sleep. But I just want you to realise that you're wasting these precious years when you could and should be having a brilliant time. You actually deserve to be having a ball – you worked so hard to get there, for God's sake, You just need to be a bit more confident. You're easily as bright and likeable as most of the other girls – so try and believe that and you will be so much happier.

If it makes you feel better right now, you end up marrying a drop dead gorgeous guy – he's as handsome as that guy you currently fancy on the 46a bus, but much more importantly, he has a beautiful soul, is incredibly good to you, and for some strange reason for which you will be eternally grateful, he loves you deeply. He's a Protestant from Belfast, by the way – far too complex to explain right now how you met, but it's a good story for another day.

His love has made you the happiest woman on earth. You might find this hard to believe, but you're never sad anymore. In fact, you're border line annoying because you are so positive and upbeat about life. 'Sad Miriam' is dead and gone. – thank the Lord.

True love is what life is all about. It saved you. Love. Nothing else matters. When you find it, cherish it. All kinds of love – between all kinds of people.

By the way, you need to get a job with a good income as you end up with a lot of mouths to feed – that's all I'm saying. I'll give you a hint – Alannah, Clara, Georgia, Jessica, Jack, Daniel, Conor and Sweet Baby James. But again, love makes it so worthwhile. They all enrich your life in too many ways to explain here.

Before I sign off, I feel it necessary to warn you of one appalling tragedy that will occur in your life. I think it would be best for you to know and then you might cope a little better than I did. Your darling sister Anne is going to die at a very young age from cancer – and there's absolutely nothing you can do to change that. So very, very sorry, but life is sometimes just inexplicably cruel. I know you will do anyway, but spend a lot of time with her – as you well know, she was - as we all said - 'the jewel in the crown' of our family. When she dies, a part of all of us dies – but she watches over us. Believe me – she really really does.

I have to sign off now – lots of things to do. I'm really quite busy, but I'll tell you all about that another day. Though in truth, it's all pretty irrelevant – the only thing that matters in life is love. Never forget that.

Look after yourself,

Miriam O Callaghan

Miriam

Dear Mary,

Please stop worrying... worrying doesn't change anything and will only make you unhappy - 'What's for you won't go by you'.

Don't be in such a hurry to get to the next place .... enjoy the moment because today is 'the Day'!

I often think of what Atticus used to say to his daughter in 'To Kill a Mockingbird'. "It's not time to worry yet."

Keep smiling.

Mary x

Mary   Kennedy

Dear Me,

This letter from the future comes to you with a sense of wonder at the difference between the person you are and the person you will become.

At 16, you are serious, studious, shy, you hate your frizzy hair and feel that everyone else is looking at you critically, and also that everyone has a better social life than you do. You study all the hours that God sends. You blush very easily and would love to have more confidence. In fact, the reason your Mam sends you to elocution lessons and Irish dancing lessons is to help give you more confidence and also to stop you turning in your toes!

Your hair drives you mad. It's frizzy and yeuch. You hate being tall and just want to be the same as everyone else. You worry about everything.

I would dearly love if you could see the life path that will unfold before you, a path of hard and successful study, a path of heartbreak and sadness with your beloved Dad dying a few short years from now, a path of love and happiness and marriage, a path of more sadness with marriage breakdown, a path of very fulfilling and stimulating work and your greatest achievement and joy, the birth of four wonderful children.

Your four children have all passed the sixteen-year mark now and you'll be delighted to know that they had more of a sense of self and confidence at that age than you did. They were and are strong, confident, caring individuals who enjoy life to the full. I wish you could have been the same.

Lots of love,

Me

Sean Hughes

What i would tell my 16 year old self is the world is not as big as i thought it was and if you meet someone with brilliant views hold on to them for dear life, more importantly try and work it out with your first love as there will never be one so sweet. The grass is not greener. All is not lost and you adjust but there is nothing so beautiful. Be proactive as others will not try and take control of your life and not wait for things to happen, finally don't ever wear yellow.

Sean Hughes

Dear Jacqueline

You are the girl who use to play under the great big palm tree in the walled garden in Ballyhorgan. You used to feel so secure there. It sheltered you from sun and rain. There you are all grown up and going to school in Caherciveen. Time to step up now. You love school but can't wait to do your Leaving Cert next year so you can go to Dublin and experience the world. You have just been to your first dance in Ballybunion while you were on holidays at your grandmother's house, and you rightly ran home when a local boy told you that you had beautiful skin. Beware of bogus chat-up lines.

Yes! You are full of confidence and you can see no barriers. You have a great interest in fashion and already make your own clothes trying to keep those seams straight on your aunt's old sewing machine. You knitted a great jumper in baby blue wool but when you washed it and hung it on the line the weight of the water made it grow to four times its original size. You can see yourself as a fashion designer and even a model. You imagine strutting down catwalks in London and Paris. Not so fast now! First you must get a job. There is a lot of talk about going into the Civil Service. I know that you have little or no interest in that. You don't even know what it is but you must take it as it is somewhere to start. You must also go to night classes, learn a language, keep up your singing, go to college of music and join a choir. You must go to The Grafton Academy to learn how to really make clothes, and learn some patience while you are there as everything doesn't just happen overnight. You must **"better yourself"** and go home every Christmas with a new coat to let all the town know that you are doing well in Dublin. You will always work for yourself as you are too opinionated to take instruction from anyone else, so when you make mistakes they will be all your own.

Take care of yourself and always be kind to others. Do good whenever you can but don't be a pushover. Use your common sense and always remember where you came from. It will stop you getting carried away and feeling that you are unique. Winning isn't always important. It's the trying that counts. Be loyal and brave, and don't live your life in fear of things that might never happen!

All the best now,

Lots of love x

Jackie

Dear 16 year old Róisín

I've thought long and hard about what to say to you. Ten scrunched up pages of my good advice mock me from the waste paper bin. Having read more self help books than you've had hot battered sausages, I'm full of good advice. But your one, wild and precious life is going to unfold exactly as it is supposed to. And to quote Juliet Turner, a songwriter you will come to admire, "you are smart enough to make it on your own".

Still, I know you have a lot of questions in that wonderfully mixed up head of yours: Will anybody ever love me? Will I always be fat and ugly? Will Paul McCartney ever marry me? Will I get the job of my dreams? Let me see. You are ♥ loved. You will be loved ♥ You are not fat and you are not ugly, no matter how many times you shout this mantra at the mirror. Macca ends up with someone else, incredibly. (It doesn't turn out too well.) The job of your dreams? Have you seen the heading on this writing paper? I know! Can you believe it?

I cannot lie to you, you lovely, funny, pretty, talented girl. (I know you hate compliments but they are true, every one.) I cannot lie. There will be difficult times. Plenty of tears. Moments when you don't think your one, wild and precious life is that precious at all. You will be your own worst enemy. You will develop some unhealthy habits, some of which I am still working on today. On the up side, no, you don't end up living in a bedsit with only stray cats and the radio for company. Bit of a relief that one, eh?

At every turn, you will find people to help you on the journey. In just a few years time you will begin to learn the truth of who you really are. Eventually, you will hear of a poet called Mary Oliver and all her words, especially these ones, will make a lot of things much cleaver. "You do not have to be good/You do not have to walk on your knees for a hundred miles through the desert, repenting/You only have to let the soft animal of your body love what it loves".

Be yourself. Love yourself. Breathe.
It's all exactly as it should be,
All my love,
38 year old Róisín ♥
xxx

Home. Dublin.

Dear Me,

I'm deeply and hopelessly in love, and just rotten at school lessons and exams. Where will this end? I'm never out of trouble with my teachers. They say I'm worthless, only fit to be a comedian.

It's true that I amuse the other boys a lot, and girls at parties, too, but not really the one I love.

Maybe I'll go to grinders' college, do the matriculation, and try to get into university that way.

Frank Kelly, B.L., B.C.L. Writer, Actor, father of seven children, and grandfather to 16 grandchildren. Where did I go wrong?

Paul Noonan

Hey Paul,

So, You are going, slightly awkward bay, it's Ok -
You'll grow into and get used to that frame...
and make the most of being able to eat stupid
amounts of food without the onset of gout.
It won't last.

Learn to type properly. Don't forget how to swim
Remember birthdays. Send more postcards.

Don't take it all so seriously. The complicated things train shtick will get you places, but they won't always be fun.

Don't pay any attention to your future self...

what does he know ☺

Dear Charlie,

I'm at me wits end with you. Why is it you keep coming home late.

Last night you didn't arrive home till just after midnight I couldn't get to sleep, wondering what type of company you are keeping.

You keep going to that God forsaken place in Mount Merrion, the Stella House Dance Hall.

Tell me, just tell me what you see in that Heatherhall, Vance Morrison, this is up to no good. Surely you'd be better off at home doing your school home work.

How many times have I told you before that if you want to get on in this life, you have to do your home work, and study hard.

If your not at that Dance Hall in Mount Merrion your spending all your time on the streets and believe no good will come of it.

The next thing you'll be doing is going out with girls — o'my God what is the world coming to.

Charlie your also spending too much time with that boy across the road, whats his name, Tony something. No good will come of it, to be honest he's a bad influence his brother has a motorbike and we know how dangerous those things are. And Charlie while I'm on the subject your also spending far too much time in the company of those three Norwegian girls whos

Dad's have Moved here to fly Rose New Planes.

Jumbo Jets S Ring Rick Ring Coll Them.

Sods only know what those Scandonian Girls get up to.

Clorlin if your going to fool around with Girls, Let it be one of our own.

Lastly Clorlin Kee Away from this New Decimal Money the Government is bringing in ... We should stick to our own pounds, shillings and Pence.

Sods only knows where all of this is going to Lead to. Re Next Ring the Government will Want us to Join Rat Ring in Europe Called the EEC.

And Remember Clorlin Rose Europeans have only one Ring on their Minds — Sex.

So Clorlin please try and Be in Before Ten O'Clock to-night. there is Some New Show on the Telly. Called the Lithe Lolo Show.

to Be Honest Clorlin I don't think this Fella.

Could Say By RUA will Last Long — He's Always talking About Sex.

Love Clorlin

Colm O'Gorman

Tara Hill, Gorey, Co. Wexford
www.colmogorman.com

27 July 2010

Dear Me,

Right now all you know is self-doubt and self-hatred. This is not because of who you are, but because of what has been done to you. I know its impossible right now for you to believe that you are worthy of love and capable of living with dignity and purpose, but you are, and that you will do so is as inevitable as the sun setting and rising. It is simply who you are.

The world in which you are forced to live right now is not yet capable of acknowledging the harm you have suffered, and the hurt you are living with is made worse by that demand upon you to be silent and compliant.
It is not your fault that your society cannot face the truth of the terrible things you and others are forced to endure and that your suffering is the price of their comfort, but that too will change.

I know too that you blame yourself for not having the courage to speak out but your silence is not silly or naïve. Sadly you are correct, to speak out would be probably dangerous for you right now. Trust your instincts, they are wise, but learn to see the difference between that wisdom and fear of what others might think of you.

Your greatest challenge in life will be to stop fearing the opinions of others, to break free of the belief that your value lies in meeting their needs and demands. You believe that to be loved you must please people, but real love is never so selfish. Love would never demand that any person deny the truth of themselves for the comfort or pleasure of another.

You will leave home soon. And when you do life will be difficult for a time, but you will emerge from all of that with a strength and certainty of purpose that you do not yet know you possess. Along the way you will meet people who want to help you. Try and be open to that, don't reject them. You will be inclined to only be open to relationships with people when you know what you can do to make them like or need you. But the people who can and will help you most are those who want nothing from you. They will help you because they value you for who you are; a human person as worthy of love and concern as any and every other. Try and trust them, they will teach you so much about how to free that deep commitment to justice and love that is also very much part of who you are.

And on love, know that it is real. I promise you this above all else; you will live a live full of and blessed by love. I promise you that you will experience freedom of heart and of spirit, that you will love with a passion that will take your breath away and that you will receive the same love in return. This will happen not because you are redeemed somehow from all that you now believe yourself to be, but because in abandoning shame and fear and discovering that you have real worth, you will finally be free to allow yourself to be loved.

All will be good, and life will be fine.

Brian Keenan

To me on my 16th birthday,

I am sending you some gifts to mark this occasion in your life. You have already determined to grow a beard, so I am sending you a shaving brush and a razor! You see beards grow thicker and fuller if you shave often. I know it seems a bit of a paradox but life will be full of such contradictions. You should enjoy them and use them to your advantage. Remember a beard can have many forms, the razor will allow you to have as many beards as suit your purpose. That's the real reason I am sending you this – so that you may have choice in how you shape yourself and the life that awaits you. A life without choice is no life at all. It is existence without meaning or value. Choice is the crown of life. Seek it out and exercise it often and, like shaving, it will make life fuller and richer for you.

I have sent you some books and also a book token. Pablo Neruda's love sonnets is one of my favourites, as is the book of psalms. They will teach you about the beauty of love and the path of adversity. I hope you will find much beauty in life, I hope you will love often and that you will find that adversity is not an obstacle but a step on the way. In the end the psalmist always rejoiced, and so should you. Life is a celebration not a trial if you choose it to be so.

Books are a great consolation and adventure but above all they teach us empathy. Without empathy your understanding of beauty, love, adversity and the whole host of emotions that make a man will be dulled and your manhood will be undeveloped. Poetry as you know is my first love – without poetry, we would not have words. I suppose that sounds like an inverted paradox too. But poetry is more than mere words. It is a magical incantation that will transport you and reveal things that will enrich you more than money. On the subject of money, I am sending you the book token to ensure you exercise your choice!

On the subject of books I have enclosed a volume of maps. It begins with copies of the earliest recorded maps of the world to the latest. See how the world has changed with knowledge. I have travelled much in my life and there remains much more I would like to see. People say that the age of miracles is over. But should you travel and love in different cultures you will find that this is not so. Cartographers were really dreamers. Imagine it, someone in a small room somewhere, drawing a picture of the world! That's a real dreamer.

Life itself is a journey. You can draw your own maps. Dream much, travel a lot and you will be able to mark the miracle spots, the love encounters and tribulations on it.

Finally I enclose a cross. No doubt you will find that the biggest paradox of all, for as you know I am not religious. But I give it to you as a kind of talisman. I think you should learn about religion (travel will help you to do this). But learn about it so that you cannot be ensnared by its proselytizers. Religion is an affair of the spirit – only you alone can know that spirit, and it will take time. Allow no-one to take it from you.

But above all, I send you this cross because it too is about choice. You see, each of us stand at the centre of the cross from which there are four different paths to take. It's a bit like a compass marking north, south, east and west. It matters not which we choose. It only matters that we do make a choice and go in that direction. Your spirit will guide you and the adventure will be wondrous!

Enjoy your birthday. Enjoy them all. Rejoice and choose joy.

Love

Brian Keenan

Dear Gerald,

La Breithe dhuit a bhean óg.

I trust your Irish is better than mine when I celebrated my 16th Birthday some 36 years ago.

I wish you nothing but continued success and happiness into the future. Having enjoyed a wonderful life so far I would suggest that you embrace each day with open arms. Be positive and remember there are many less fortunate than your good-self. Honesty always prevails and there is great satisfaction in helping and sharing with others. Always remain positive and true to your beliefs.

DRAYTON MANOR,
THREE MILE WATER,
WICKLOW.

Don't be Influenced by a small minority
who are unhappy with their lot in life.
Enjoy each day!
As you know I am good friends with your
Mother and Father, Patricia and Gerald, so don't
be afraid to follow their advice and path through life!
Share different Experiences with them and enjoy every minute.
I had great fun bringing my own parents to Rock concerts,
football matches, theatre, circus etc! The memories will last
forever. Don't lose the Importance of Inter personal Relationships.

On that note please give my very best to your
wonderful Brother, Richard, and your gorgeous Sister Adrienne!

I finish by saying, continue to enjoy every moment of
your life, and remember the Joy of giving and sharing with
others like the many people around us experience every day.

Sorry we cannot be with you this evening!

Lots of Love
    Gerald
        (also on behalf of Kirsten and Russ)

Jennifer Johnston

Hi there, the words echo back through the years, bumping off ~~then~~ walls and disasters, marriages and divorce, deaths and births, tears and laughter, work and idleness — now that is something I have always meant to have a word with you about. Idleness. You want to watch that, guard against it. It comes too easily to you. Think of being as idle at eighty as you are at sixteen. It doesn't bear thinking about I hear you mutter. But this I would one say to you, young one that you are, pull your socks up, learn how to work before it is too late; otherwise you will end up like me — amiable, yes, by all means, but soooo bloody idle. As you so correctly muttered it doesn't bear thinking about.

with love

Jennifer Johnston

1945

Colum McCann

Dear Me

Weren't you lucky that Ben Kiely wrote a story that blew your heart sideways? Weren't you lucky to have found that poem by Seamus Heaney? Weren't you lucky that there was a Richard Brautigan book on the stairs? Weren't you lucky that your father brought home books and then went down the garden?

Weren't you lucky that your good folks were such good folks? Weren't you lucky for that sandwich that rainy Thursday afternoon? Weren't you lucky to hear the white radiator ticking in the cold? Weren't you lucky that you found out that luck is the understanding of other people's stories? Weren't you lucky to be led towards the notion that life is constantly unfinished? Weren't you lucky that you wanted to have some regrets?

Weren't you lucky that you were allowed to leave with the right passport? Weren't you lucky that you spent so many idle summers worried about idle summers? Weren't you lucky that you hated the face of Margaret Thatcher that summer of 1981? Weren't you lucky that you knew there were 16-year-old kids in Newcastle too? Weren't you lucky that you were not allowed to throw bricks? Weren't you lucky to think that there were planes?

Weren't you lucky that it was complicated? Weren't you lucky that you knew what a certain amount of sadness was? Weren't you lucky to be away from the barricade? Weren't you lucky that you could see the beauties too? Weren't you lucky that you had your legs? Weren't you lucky you had your shoes? Weren't you lucky that you had some places to go? Weren't you lucky that there was luck? Weren't you lucky that you didn't put too many manners on your life? Weren't you lucky you took a chance?

Weren't you lucky that the woman you were to love wasn't there yet? Weren't you lucky you spent a long time finding her? Weren't you lucky there were so many roads to go? Weren't you lucky you took some wrong turns? Weren't you lucky there was so much in front of you? Weren't you lucky to dream that one day soon you'd be three-times sixteen? Weren't you lucky to have the word 'luck' carved on the aorta of your heart? Weren't you lucky to think that you deserved it, when, truly, everyone else gave it? Weren't you lucky to think that, one day, despite it all, you could still be this lucky? Hey, aren't we lucky that you're still looking? Aren't you lucky to be able, still, to walk away from me now?

Colum

Dear Me,

Life is full of ups and downs, but if you keep trying you will succeed. As the only boy to be taking home economics in school it may not be the most popular thing to do, but cooking is wonderful and will give you great rewards in all areas of your life, and stick with the sewing the shirt you will make will have its uses, even if it is for polishing!

Love everything you do, follow your passion and work hard. Be respectful to everyone you meet, remember those who help you along the way and help them back in return. Keep focused on what you want to achieve and know that everybody takes knocks but there is always another way to get to your goal.

Don't forget to have fun, if you love what you do it will always be fun, enjoy travelling and the experiences you'll have.

From

Neven Maguire

MacNean House & Restaurant, BLA

Tel: 071-9853022   Fax: 071-9853404   Email: INFO@MACNEANRESTAU

Brian Kennedy

Dear 16-year-old me,

I hope you don't mind me writing to you from your future. You're still in Belfast I know, on the Falls Road, and are quietly wondering to yourself whether you'll ever get out alive. Well the good news is that you do. Not only that, but you actually end up travelling the world for a living and getting to be a proper singer after all. You even become a published author – hard to believe I know, when you are about to fail your English exam.

I'm tempted to tell you not to bother applying for those three A-level exams at a girls' school because your own St Paul's School – all boys – couldn't offer any further education, but I know only too well how stubborn you can be. At least you gave it a few months before you dropped out. So you're at a crossroads, but the music is around the corner.

Don't worry fella, the summer that's coming will change everything. You're going to start by cutting your dark boring hair and bleaching it white in an effort to look nothing like yourself (mission accomplished, even with those eyebrows!), and it's really the first step in cutting the ties of who you once were and grabbing at your independence.

If I could sit with you now in a café in the centre of town where you might just have enough money for a cup of milky tea and a bun, I'd be itching to tell you that in the future you won't feel as invisible and small as you do now. I don't want to give everything away, but if you look over to the City Hall where the punks hang out and sneer and smoke, I wonder can you picture yourself as a grown man, on stage with another Belfast son called Van Morrison and the then President of America, Bill Clinton, and the first lady, Hilary, who have come to switch on the Christmas lights as a sign of solidarity and peace? Your voice will ring out into the city air in harmony with Van as around 90,000 people stand in the freezing cold watching from the street below, along with an estimated TV audience of about one billion. History in the making, but as I say there's more of that to come and I'm not telling you everything.

Most of all though Brian, my 16-year-old self, I want to put my arms around you and hold you close and tell you everything will be OK. We both know only too well that you have a secret that you're terrified of on one hand, while still trying to work it out on the other. You grow up to write a song called 'Get On With Your Short Life' and it's your own advice you should take. I'll say it for you, you happen to love men in the most natural profound way that you know and it terrifies you in these teenage years. There are many women that you grow up to care about deeply, but in the still of the night it's *his* arms that will only bring peace to your heart. You'll find him, Brian, when you least expect him to call, and when you do it will feel like he was always there. I promise. Don't worry, you'll have some of the best sex in your life along the way too.

So, teenage Brian, get out of your own way and let yourself be who you are. Some people call it queer, others gay. Call it what you like, but for you it's who you really are and I'd love to tell you to not waste so much time in denial about it, but we all have our journeys to take at our own pace. Take your time, but breathe deeper and stop being so hard on yourself. I'm sorely tempted to give you the lottery numbers and some football results but they never were and still aren't passions of yours. Music stays at your very centre and that is something to be proud of and to continue to feel privileged about. You're in for a rollercoaster ride make no mistake, but I wouldn't – and you wouldn't – have it any other way.

Love, Older Brian xx

Dublin 2010

Feargal Quinn

Senator Feargal Quinn

SEANAD ÉIREANN
Leinster House
Dublin 2
Ireland
Tel: +353 (1) 618 3410
Fax: +353 (1) 618 4625

President
SUPERQUINN
Sutton Cross
Dublin 13
Ireland
Tel: +353 (1) 839 5198
Email: himself@feargalquinn.ie
Website: www.feargalquinn.ie

Dear Feargal,

I remember you well, and how anxious you were to make sure you never let your parents down in any way, both in your studies and in your sporting activities. Keep that concern high in the years ahead because your good name is very important — much more important than any money you earn.

In later years, you will meet, and become friendly with, a Japanese business man called Masatoshi Ito — he opened his first shop when you were 15 years of age (i.e. last year) in 1952.

On one occasion, I asked Ito-san how he became so successful — his chain now has 14,500 branches — and he quoted a message that has guided him throughout his career: 'Whether you believe you can or whether you believe you can't, you are right'. Its a message I'd live you to remember going through life. If you have belief in yourself, you can achieve a great deal and you will always win out against a competitor who does not have that confidence.

When you decide to go into business — and you will be 23 when you open your first shop — keep in mind the advice your father gave you. He ran Red Island Holiday Camp in Skerries and was always guided by 'The Boomerang Principle' — that the objective in business is not to maximise the profit from a customer on this visit, but to make yes sure that the customer has such a good experience that he/she will come back again. In other words, look to the long term.

And above all, remember that success in life is being happy at home. Enjoy the company of your wife and children — and grandchildren!

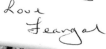

Love
Feargal

Dear John,

When I think of you it is almost as I would of a
son. I know there are things about which I know more
than you do, but — alas — one of the things I know
most certainly is that I cannot hope to alert you to
the consequences of your relative unknowing. Nor do
I necessarily wish to do so. If I were your father,
I might say, "I cannot live your life for you."
The trouble is that I have already done so — well,
perhaps optimistically, half to two-thirds of your
life. This changes everything.

I remember a gauche, gangly youth with long hair
who had certain clear ideas about things. I have to
tell you that almost everything you knew was wrong.
I could waste my precious 500 words by telling you
things with a view to saving you time and heartbreak,
but that too would be a fruitless direction. I am
the consequence of mistakes you have yet to make.

Instead, all I would like to say is that I feel
intimately connected with you in every moment.
I look back towards you, through the few instants
of space time that separate us, and draw from you a
sense of my bearings. I measure the journey that
I have made — the one you must yet make — and from
that draw a sense of what is left for us both to
undertake. The news is not so good. I am still
gauche and not ungangly. I still have long hair.
I know minutely more than you do, but that
"knowledge", too, informed mainly by the mistakes,
is probably still all wrong. If we are working off
the three-score-and-ten, then I have much to
discover, on behalf of us both, in fifteen years
(soberingly, rather less than half the time that
separates you from me).

All I can tell you of what I've learned is that
it's all a mystery. Or, far more likely, a Mystery.
It makes sense, but not as you imagine. It's not a
movie or a book, and neither of these will afford
you more than the odd glimpse of guidance. The
destination is no clearer by virtue of being nearer,
but the sense of a destination grows all the time.
As I remember, you have a highly developed sense of
the absurd, but I seem to remember also that you are
to lose that for a time, which may be the first real
mistake. The root of your greatest errors will be a
brief but unfortunate lapsing into the general
tendency to take everything at face value. Look
around. Look at yourself. How can it be as they say?
Wonder is the only way.

The picture is growing, but so painfully slowly that
it seems hopeless to imagine it will complete itself
in time. To be truthful, my best expectation is for
a gauche, gangly, long-haired seventy-year-old John
who will look back at both of us and laugh himself
to death.

Good wishes across the puddle of comedy and time.

August '10

To my 16 year old self,

I can honestly say that I really like you. In fact, I would happily be your friend. Despite the restrictions of your awkward, transitionary age and the daily mundane routine of school, in many ways you are more liberated than the 26 year old me. Little did you know that in a mere 8 years time, your life as you know it would be changed unimaginably, your days and weeks ruled by daunting contracts, long-haul flights and worldwide media interest.

You are just the right side of naughty; happy to skip school in favour of balmy days on Killiney Beach, snog spotty teenage boys at sweaty discos and take swigs of cheap wine in somebody's back garden, yet the idea of getting completely plastered, taking anything illegal or having sex with a stranger are utterly outside your realm of consideration. You have emerged from that gangly, angular 14 year-old body, with its braided smile and coltish legs, and are really blossoming into a young woman. You are a creative and hardworking student and a competitive, talented athlete, with a plethora of medals, trophies and rosettes displayed proudly at home.

With frequent weekend trips on the DART into town, and with them the opportunity to explore Dublin City sans parents, your sense of individuality and freedom is developing rapidly. With it, your sense of your own sexuality is being realised; you unashamedly flirt with every cute boy you see and teenage crushes end as quickly as they begin! It's exciting to explore the big bad world with your friends, but you ultimately love returning to the comfort of your home and your loving family.

Though I am very happy with how my life has panned out so far, I would love to walk in your shoes for just one more day; to relive the thrills and excitements of those small things that seem so huge in your teenage mind. The best advice I can offer is to enjoy every little second of it. Let your body, mind and soul grow and develop together, don't let anybody inhibit your progress. Even the smallest gesture or cruel word from another can crush a fragile self-esteem. Be a confident, strong and ambitious young woman and work HARD for every academic and sporting achievement. Believe me, it will stand to you.

Stay true to yourself, girl, and keep up the fight. I'm really proud of you.

Rosanna Davison
x

Dear Christy, Your heading into adulthood now so remember issues that seem like the end of the world now you will laugh at their insignificance when your older, and if I was to give you good advice it is, all your enemies wont have danger tatoo'd on their foreheads everybody who smiles at you is not necessarily your mate. Good luck your gonna need it

Christy Dignam
16 years

Dear Maeve,

It all looks a bit bleak.

It's summer 1956 and the living is far from easy. You have just left school; the youngest in your form, the quickest to answer questions in class, the slowest to climb the hills on a picnic, the last to be picked for any kind of team, way at the back when it came to being asked to dance. Bad start, what lies ahead except more humiliation?

University is going to be another stage where the race goes to the swift, the pretty, the thin.

Oh, I would love to tell you how wrong this is. To calm your poor big anxious heart, to beg you not to try so hard, or worry so much. You will find that no one is watching you, no one at all. They are all, like you, worrying about themselves. What hours and days of freedom you would have if you were told this!

Except of course you wouldn't have believed it, no matter how clearly it was explained. It only dawns after years of liking people, loving them and needing them without even being remotely aware what they look like.

That's Real Life but at sixteen we aren't ready for it.

Maeve Binchy

Maeve Binchy

PADDY MOLONEY

July 2010

Dear younger Paddy,

Here are some points that I will offer to you as a teenager and hope that you take one or two to heart......

-   Don't tell your mother you have a bad cold and you need to stay home from school, just so you can play the old cracked up 78's on the wind up gramophone, she'll know........

-   Try not to stay up too late having "House Hooleys" (house dances) the night before a pipes competition or you'll be sure to come in 3rd or 4th place instead of 1st.

-   You'll probably yearn for a motorbike, forget it, you'll freeze to death

-   After you've been to the cinema with your girlfriend, don't lie and say you're going straight home and go to a live music session instead until the wee hours, you will be found out.

-   Eat the crusts off your bread as you'll learn later that you like it best.

-   You don't need to be upset when some of your friends mock you for playing the pipes or traditional music as they will one day be giving you a standing ovation at Carnegie Hall.

-   Live your dreams as they can come true, anything is possible if you really work at it.

Good Luck!

Slightly Older Paddy

Andrea Roche

Dear Me,

I know at times you feel that your Mum is strict with you but please be patient with her, what she is doing is for your own good and because she loves you.

As life goes on your mother will be your your greatest friend and will inspire you in so many ways. You will learn, in time, all the sacrifices that she has made for you, so try to tell her every day how much you love her.

You are funny, loyal, sensitive and honest. Stay that way and you will always be surrounded by good friends and loved ones which is so important in life.

Don't wish your birthdays away: turning 18 is not everything. One of these days you will realise how quickly time goes by so enjoy every moment of your youth.

Love your friends and family with all your heart. Try to forgive easily and not hold grudges - the people that love the most won't always be here on earth.

Stay the way you are now - friendly, hardworking, humble and always have a smile for everyone and you will go a long way.

XX
Andrea

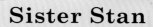

Dear Treasa,

(I'll call you Treasa for now – but you won't always be known by that name!)

At the moment, you're thinking a lot about the present and the future, and wondering what path you should take. From all you have read so far about the poverty in Ireland and around the world, you're thinking of how you can somehow become involved in working with those poor and vulnerable........well my best advice to you is to just follow your instinct and go for it! Go for it with your whole heart and being.

The road you will travel in your life in the next fifty-odd years will be amazing – and the questions and wonderings you have right now are all valuable and worthwhile – learn everything you can and question everything you can and give yourself 100% happily to what you want to do because it is the right thing for you.

Your family and certainly your circle of friends will expand and grow hugely – to include some truly wonderful people that you'd hardly be able to imagine at the moment.

Just keep doing exactly what you're doing and trust in your own instinct and gut feeling that what you want to change and achieve can be done.

I wish you the best of luck with it all – and enjoy the journey!!

Stan

Stan
(you'll understand in a few years...)

20th July 2010

Dear (older) me,

How's the future going? I've changed my mind so much these past few months about what I want to do after school. Right now I hope your a doctor, Any chance of a hint from the future? If they've invented time travel by then please do =D Hope your year travelling was as amazing as you thought it was going to be. Did you go to all all of the places on the list like Paris, Tokyo, Italy Hong Kong, Milan, Thailand.....
The list is endless. I hope the year in Oz was everything you thought it would be and more I'll try and learn to swim so it won't be as much of a challenge living there.

Is the Computer Club still there? How's everyone? Has Ciarán been committed yet? If it's still running tell everyone I said hello! I hope you still talk to everyone from Gurteen, Maybe even still go down every summer? Remember the first year you went down? It was the best week ever (well that I know about) Ask Kelly if she remembers Ethan and Julie. Did you get your dream of owning a big house, owning a Bugatti Veyron and marrying Robert Pattinson? Ha let me know how that one goes :L Have they managed to bring people back from the dead yet? Is there hover cars? Can people be turned invisible? I really hope your still in contact with some of your old friends like Kelly 'coz she's the best and Kavanagh 'coz he's

20th July 2010

friggin' hilarious!!. Hope Katie and
Shannon are okay and still as mad
as ever!
Here's a couple of things that should
bring a smile to your face:
♫ Lean on me ♫
Mmm yesh some nice vaniller!
26
You ate my cookie?!!
Are you for serdious?
Florry had banoffee on her shoe.
Who owns ye?
The hacka the hacka yi! =D
Bet down like lino, no actually under
the lino
♫ As we go on, we remember ♫
♫ We are St. Trinians ♫
   Hope that brought back a few
memories. Tell everyone I said hello
            Lots of love
         Your 16 year old self
            Rebecca xxx.

Our 16-year-old
Rebecca, to her
future self

Writing to Yourself

If you've loved reading the letters here, why not write your own? Use the following pages to compose your note, and then scan and send it to withlovefrommetome@josephgalliano.co.uk and we'll post it on our blog at www.withlovefrommetome.com

You could also sign up to the With Love From Me to Me Facebook page and post your letters and photos there, and follow us on Twitter.

.... at sixteen years of age

26-8-10

Dear younger me,
   23 years from now (when you are)
please PLEASE remember to thank the
many people who have helped make
this fabulous project work — The
Contributors, those who have helped
me reach them, the publishers,
distributors, charity and most
importantly... The Readers!
   We wouldn't have this
   book without them.
      With love from me...
         To me joe Gallino
            X

Acknowledgements

With love, from me... to you

The editor wishes to extend his heartfelt thanks to all of you who have made this wonderful project possible. Thank you most especially to all of the contributors and their parents who have given so kindly of their time and private material and let us glimpse through such an intimate window into their lives. A long thank-you letter in the mail to Miriam O'Callaghan, who so generously fitted us into her ferocious schedule. In no particular order and almost certainly with startling omissions, letters of commendation and gratitude are in the post for: Alan Johnston, Maria Dickenson, David O'Callaghan, Charlotte Robertson, Eoin McHugh, Brian Langan, Kate Tolley, Katrina Whone, Phil Lord, Nick Avery, Simon Hess, Aislinn Casey, Liam O'Dwyer, Sabina Cotter, Claire O'Connor, Christine Fitzpatrick, Evelyn Byrne, John Nesbitt, Sinead McPhillips, Ian Young, Noel Kelly, Niamh Kirwan, David Jaymes, Moira Bellas, Fred Mellor, Stuart Bell, Murray Chalmers, Sarah Pritchard, Alan Nierob, Declan Heeney, Louise Page, Sophie Austin, Dallas Smith, Paul Smith, Sarah Owen, Alison Owen, Darren Smith, Gill Waters, Eavan Kenny, Ami Burke, Lisa Thomas, Nathalie Laurent-Marke, Piers Atkinson, Margy Kenny, Emily Shanks, Anna Morel, Vittoria Colonna, Claire Nightingale, Bill Cullen, Hannah Gould, Terry Hughes, Steve Macklam, Michelle Findlay, Michelle Kass, Andrew Mills, Brian Lougheed, Caitlin Raynor, Vivienne Smith, Aoife Sullivan, Aileen Carville, Keira-Eva Mooney, Geraldine Kennedy, Luke Ingram, Sam Cook, Sarah Conroy, Mark Downing, Jane Blackley, Kathleen Clarke, Barry Gaster, Norrie McGregor, Paul Howard, Olga Slutskaya, Dan Oggly, Liza Geddes, Valerie Morrison, Gareth Davies, Sara Lee, Eavan Kenny, Lynda O'Keeffe, Karen Hodges, Denis Vaughan, Mike Perry, Joseph O'Reilly, The Galliano's, The O'Neil's, Kristian Digby and his friends, especially Stephen, Jessica, Adeana, Jon, Sally, Sarah, Gareth, Tracey, Mark, Fen, but most of all, Mark Stuart Doig...patience of a saint. Thank you.

This book is dedicated with love to Winifred O'Neil 1918-2010

The Irish Youth Foundation was founded in 1985 by Norma Smurfit to support children and young people from disadvantaged communities in Ireland, and to help them overcome adversity in their lives.

The Irish Youth Foundation has many heroes – young people who have overcome the barriers life has given them and who want to succeed, in whatever ways are best for them and their communities. One hero is Rebecca Nolan, so please read her letter. If you would like to know more about the Irish Youth Foundation and how you can help, please go to www.iyf.ie

Our Driving Passion: To build a brighter future for vulnerable children and young people.

What we do: We raise funds for local and community groups across the island of Ireland.

Who we support: Innovative 'grassroots' projects run by passionate professionals and dedicated volunteers who understand and care about children and young people.

How we do it: There are five key areas through which we provide opportunities for children and young people in Ireland to succeed:

Education

After-school and homework clubs have been a cornerstone of our work for the past twenty-five years. These clubs give children positive learning experiences as well as addressing their need for affirmation, belonging and self-esteem.

Play!

Children love to play and have fun – we all do. We support summer programmes so children and young people remain active and engaged, and can learn new skills for positive recreation.

Expression

Everything from dancing to singing, music making, DJing, rapping, story-telling, creative writing and more. We also support special projects, such as horse riding and animal care, for children with disabilities.

Leadership

Young people take leadership when it is offered and we have devised programmes with our partners that give real opportunities for young people to lead, to shine, and to care about the communities they live in.

Prevention

Some young people struggle with drugs, alcohol and anti-social behaviour while often living in dysfunctional or broken families. We help when we can but most of our efforts are directed at prevention – trying to intervene before the damage is done.